RIVER THA
SHIPPING
SINCE 2000
PASSENGER SHIPS,
FERRIES, HERITAGE
SHIPPING AND MORE

MALCOLM BATTEN

Acknowledgements and Bibliography

Brown, Paul, *Historic ships: The Survivors* (Stroud: Amberley, 2010).

Clapham, Phoebe, *Thames Path in London* (London, Aurum, 2018).

Clegg, W. Paul, *Docks and Ports: 2 – London* (Shepperton: Ian Allen, 1987).

Hall, Nick, 'London's Pride' (in *Ships Monthly*, May 2007).

Lunn, Geoff, *Port of London Shipping: An Era of Change* (Stroud: Tempus, 2004).

Lunn, Geoff, *Port of London Through Time* (Stroud: Amberley, 2011).

Ormston, John M., *The Five Minute Crossing: The Tilbury – Gravesend Ferries* (Thurrock, Thurrock Local History Society, 1998).

Tucker, Joan, *Ferries of the Lower Thames* (Stroud, Amberley, 2010).

Wiltshire, Andrew, *Thames Tugs in Colour* (Portishead: Bernard McCall, 2017).

Details of current shipping can be found on various websites including www.shipspotting.com.

First published 2020

Amberley Publishing
The Hill, Stroud
Gloucestershire, GL5 4EP

www.amberley-books.com

Copyright © Malcolm Batten, 2020

The right of Malcolm Batten to be identified as the Author of this work has been asserted in accordance with the Copyrights, Designs and Patents Act 1988.

ISBN 978 1 4456 9071 1 (print)
ISBN 978 1 4456 9072 8 (ebook)

British Library Cataloguing in Publication Data.
A catalogue record for this book is available from the British Library.

Origination by Amberley Publishing.
Printed in the UK.

Contents

Introduction

The City of London owes its existence and development to the River Thames. The site was originally chosen as a settlement by the Romans, who named it Londinium. The location was chosen as the nearest point to the estuary that the Romans could bridge the river with the technology at their disposal. The building of the first London Bridge then dictated the shape of the emerging settlement. Becoming a barrier to any ships that couldn't pass under it, it meant that the wharves, warehouses and all other amenities associated with shipping came to be sited along the river to the east of the bridge. For several hundred years after the Romans left, London Bridge remained the only bridge in an expanding London. Other bridges would be added to the west, but it would not be until Tower Bridge opened in 1894 that a bridge was built to the east. This would then remain unique until the Dartford bridge opened in 1991 – still the only bridge across the river east of Tower Bridge, and all because of the need to provide clearance for shipping.

But take a look at the River Thames in East London now and you would think that it is commercially dead. Where once the banks of the river were lined with riverside wharves, from the Upper Pool between Tower and London bridges down to Woolwich, these have nearly all been replaced by or converted to luxury apartments. The London Docks network, including the St Katherine Docks, the East and West India Docks, the Surrey Docks on the south side of the river, and the mighty 'Royals', once the largest expanse of enclosed dockland in the world, had all closed by 1983 and have since been redeveloped as Docklands, with a financial centre, London City Airport, the University of East London, houses, shopping and other amenities.

However, the commercial life of the river didn't die – it just moved downriver. The advent of new cargo-handling technology, in particular the development of container ships and Roll-on, Roll-off ferries, led to the Port of London Authority deciding that future investment should be concentrated downstream at their other port at Tilbury, as the existing docks were not suited to such traffic.

The London International Cruise Terminal, alongside the pier for the ferry to Gravesend, continues to handle cruise ships. During the summer months, some of these also travel upriver to moor at Greenwich, or venture through Tower Bridge to berth alongside HMS *Belfast* in the Pool of London. Also coming right up to the Pool of London or berthing in the West India Dock are vessels on courtesy visits, often foreign naval craft. At Woolwich fast commuter ferries to London cross paths with the Woolwich Free Ferry, while a passenger ferry still links Gravesend with Tilbury.

From Greenwich to central London the commuter ferries share the river with the excursion craft that still convey tourists along this part of London's river.

The Thames in London is home to a number of heritage vessels. Tourists flock to visit HMS *Belfast* in the Upper Pool and the *Cutty Sark* at Greenwich. The marina at St Katherine Dock usually houses some of the traditional Thames spritsail barges that once worked much of the coastal traffic from Essex and Suffolk. These, and other visiting craft, can sometimes be seen sailing on the river.

This book takes a look at some of the varying passenger shipping that has worked on or visited the Thames since 2000. Also featured are the various craft that service the port such as ship-handling tugs, pilot launches, bunkering tankers, etc. There are visiting ships on courtesy calls. Sailing ships such as sail training ships are included; and heritage shipping both locally based, including the traditional Thames sailing barges, and visiting vessels also feature. A companion book will cover the various types of cargo shipping to be seen.

The closure of most of the upriver commercial wharves and the subsequent creation of the Thames Path has provided many viewpoints along the river. There is now a riverside path on both sides of the river from Hampton Court, via Central London, to Island Gardens, Greenwich, on the north side and the Thames Barrier on the south side, running alongside the riverbank for much of the way. The Thames Path extension continues on the north bank to the entrance of Bow Creek, while on the south side it continues from the Thames Barrier past Woolwich and Erith to Crayford Ness. Pleasure craft run from Central London to Greenwich, and commuter ferries on to Woolwich. However, there is no regular passenger service beyond Woolwich. For many people, the only chance to photograph locations beyond Gravesend from the river is on the annual season of visits by the paddle steamer *Waverley*, now owned by the Paddle Steamer Preservation Society. For around two weeks each September/October the *Waverley* operates on the Thames, running excursions to/from Tower Pier to Southend, the Thames forts, up the Medway, or on to Whitstable, Clacton or beyond. Some of the photographs in this book have been taken on such excursions and readers are strongly recommended to patronise these tours. Not only does it make for a great day out, you will be helping to keep this grand old lady of the sea, the last sea-going paddle steamer in the world, afloat and carrying passengers. Unfortunately, the *Waverley* has had to be taken out of service and will not be working any tours in 2019 as she needs a new boiler. Details of the appeal to raise the £2.3 million of funds needed for this and the progress in undertaking the work can be found on their website www.waverleyexcursions.co.uk.

All photographs are by the author except where stated.

Note that in a few cases background 'clutter' such as chimneys and wind turbines have been digitally removed.

Flashback

In the 1970s many of the cruise ships sailing from Tilbury were Russian-owned – at a time when the Iron Curtain was still in place. This is the *Mikhail Kalinin* departing from the landing stage. Note the hammer and sickle emblem on the funnel, found on most Russian shipping at the time. They were operated by the London-based CTC Lines (later CTC Cruise Lines). (Photo by Reg Batten)

An earlier generation of Woolwich ferries, represented by the steam-powered paddle ferry *Will Crooks* (1930, 621 tonnes). Four coke-fired ferries were built by the J. Samuel White shipyard at Cowes between 1922 and 1930 – the *Squires*, *Gordon*, *Will Crooks* and *John Benn*. They were replaced in 1963 by the diesel ferries that were themselves replaced in 2018. (Photo by Reg Batten)

The Port of London Authority had their own fleet of tugs for manoeuvring ships within the Royal Docks. This is the *Plangent*, bringing a vessel through from the lock into King George V Dock. She was built in 1951 and worked for the PLA until 1986, when she was sold to new owners in Greece. (Photo by Reg Batten)

No longer to be found on the Thames is the former Clyde paddle steamer *Caledonia*, built in 1934 for the London, Midland & Scottish Railway. Withdrawn in 1969, she was bought by Bass Charington and was converted to a pub/restaurant named *Old Caledonia*, moored close to Waterloo Bridge. Unfortunately, she was destroyed by fire in April 1980 and was later towed away for scrap. Her steam engines survive at the Hollycombe Steam Museum near Liphook. (Photo by Reg Batten)

Passenger Shipping

Cruise Ships

Cruise ships come up the Thames to Tilbury all year round, but to London only from about Easter to September. There are three locations they reach. At Tilbury is the London International Cruise Terminal, formerly the Tilbury Landing Stage Terminal. This opened in 1930. After the war it saw both the first emigration of '£10 Poms' to Australia in 1947 and the first wave of Caribbean immigrants on the *Empire Windrush* in 1948. In 1989 the terminal was adapted for cruise ships and renamed. The terminal was originally rail-served by the adjacent Tilbury Riverside station but this was closed in 1992 as the ocean liner traffic had ended. In London ships moor at either Greenwich Ship Tier, close to Greenwich pier, or in the Upper Pool alongside HMS *Belfast*. This location involves passing through Tower Bridge, with the experience of a bridge lift for the passengers. In 2013 Enderby Riverside Limited gained planning permission for a new international cruise terminal at Enderby Wharf in Greenwich, to open in 2016. However, this brought about a lot of local opposition on the grounds of emissions from the ships' engines, as a shore to ship power supply was not being provided. Eventually the scheme was abandoned.

One of the main users of the London International Cruise Terminal at Tilbury Landing Stage is Cruise & Maritime Voyages (CMV), whose vessels can be seen all year round. The *Marco Polo* [Nassau] is seen on 4 August 2013. A veteran built in 1965, in earlier times she would also have visited Tilbury when under her original Russian ownership as the *Alexandr Pushkin*, although she has been much rebuilt and had her superstructure lengthened since.

Seen from the landing stage, used also by the Tilbury Ferry, *Marco Polo* is tied up awaiting departure time as Maersk container ship *Maersk Bali* is escorted past to the Northfleet Hope container terminal.

It is 18 May 2014 and *Marco Polo* sets off on another cruise. The Svitzer tug that has assisted her is returning to base.

Another of the CMV ships, the *Columbus* [Nassau] is on the landing stage on 15 May 2019. She was built in France in 1988 as the *Sitmar FairMajesty*, and has had several owners and refits since, most recently on acquisition by CMV in 2017. The clock tower of the cruise terminal can be seen to the left.

The most recent acquisition by CMV Voyages is the *Vasco Da Gama*, which first visited Tilbury on 6 June 2019. This was originally the *Statendam* (1993) with Holland America Line and was a regular visitor to Tilbury under their ownership.

The *Arielle* is on the stage on an earlier occasion on 2 September 2007. She was built in 1971 in Finland for Royal Caribbean Cruise Lines as *Nordic Prince*. When photographed, she was owned by Louis Cruise Lines, Cyprus, as the *Aquamarine*, but was on charter to Transocean Tours as the *Arielle*.

One of the largest ships to berth at the Tilbury Landing Stage is the *Norwegian Pearl* of Norwegian Cruise Line, which called there on 23 May 2019 and again in June. Launched in 2006, she can carry 2,394 passengers.

Other cruise ships continue upriver to berth at Greenwich or the Upper Pool. Approaching Woolwich on her way to the Upper Pool on 29 May 2019 is the *Silver Wind* (1994) of Silversea Voyages. She has been a regular seasonal visitor, along with *Silver Cloud*, *Silver Shadow* and *Silver Whisper*.

The *Europa* [Nassau] passes through the Thames flood barrier, at Silvertown, on the way outwards from Greenwich in June 2014. Built in 1999, she is owned by the German company Hapag-Lloyd Cruises.

An interesting visitor to Greenwich Ship Tier on 29 May 2006 was the Japanese-owned *Nippon Maru* [Tokyo]. She entered service in 1990 and is owned by Mitsui OSK Passenger Line Ltd.

A stern view of the *Amadea* [Nassau] at Greenwich on 14 August 2010. She was built in Japan in 1991 as the *Asuka* and is now operated under charter by Phoenix Reisen of Germany.

The World [Nassau] is a residential cruise ship, offering 110 apartments and eighty-eight guest suites aboard. Owned by ResidenSea Ltd, she called at Greenwich on her maiden voyage in April 2002 and has been back again since, including here in September 2007 and, most recently, in July 2019.

Occasionally a ship may moor in the Lower Pool, east of Tower Bridge, if the Upper Pool berth is unavailable. This seems to have been the case with Silja Line's *Silja Opera* on 9 September 2005.

Arriving at Tower Bridge on 8 May 2017 is the French-owned *Le Boreal*. She dates from 2010 and is owned by Compagnie du Ponant. The passengers have amassed on deck to photograph the bascule bridge opening for the ship to pass through.

On 17 May 2010 the *C. Columbus* [Nassau] is being towed backwards through the bridge. She will then be turned by the tugs in the Lower Pool for her journey back downriver. The times of arrival and departure and hence bridge lifts are governed entirely by the tides and not convenience for road traffic – a lift during the peak hour will cause disruption for some twenty minutes. Then there will be a second lift before or afterwards for the tugs fetching the ship or returning after berthing it.

On 12 June 2008 *Prince Albert II* is being towed stern-first by tug *Adsteam Redbridge* towards Tower Bridge. Owned by Silversea, she was built as an expedition cruise ship capable of sailing in some of the remotest destinations, including both polar regions. In 2011 she was renamed *Silver Explorer*.

By contrast, *Seabourn Legend*, seen here in 2014 moored alongside HMS *Belfast*, has been turned on her inward journey so she is already facing the sea for her journey back down the Thames. She was owned by Seabourn Cruise Line until she was sold in 2015.

During the London Olympic Games in 2012, some cruise ships were employed for the duration. German ship *Deutschland* [Neustadt in Holstein] was anchored in West India Dock, where she was used as a hotel and for corporate hospitality by the German authorities. Here she was on 27 July. Built in 1998 and owned by Peter Deilmann Reederei, she and the *Berlin* have been regular visitors to the Thames.

Two other ships, the *Braemar* of Fred Olsen Line and *Gemini*, were moored in Royal Albert Dock to provide accommodation for the hundreds of bus drivers brought in from all over the country to drive buses on park & ride services and to transport the 'Games Family' – athletes, media, sponsors, etc. – between venues. This view was taken from the Docklands Light Railway on 15 July and shows the two vessels along with many of the buses parked up on the quayside.

Commuter Ferries

Various attempts at a commuter ferry service between Greenwich and Central London were tried from the 1970s to 1990s without success. But the new century saw near services, new piers being built and success. White Horse Fast Ferries started a service in 2000 from the new £1.5 million Blackfriars pier to Canary Wharf. They also ran a Greenwich–Millennium Dome connection for the Millennium exhibition. But as this exhibition failed to attract visitors, that service ended early and White Horse filed for bankruptcy. A commuter ferry service was started by Collins River Enterprises in 1999 with the *Storm Clipper*, a sixty-two-seater catamaran running from Canary Wharf to Embankment every half hour in the morning and evening peaks. This was followed by the similar *Sky Clipper* and, in 2002, by the much larger *Hurricane Clipper*, enabling all-day operation. This company developed into Thames Clippers, with peak hour services extended to Woolwich Arsenal Pier from 2005 and westwards to Chelsea in 2006. Now they have nineteen vessels, carrying over 4 million passengers a year, of which some 70 per cent are commuters. Services are integrated into the Transport for London pricing and the Oyster card ticketing system. In 2006 the company was acquired by Anschutz Entertainment Group, who also own the O2 (formerly the Millennium Dome).

Back in January 2000 and White Horse Ferries were using their trimaran vessel *Wilkins Micawber* (1996) on a shuttle service between Greenwich Pier and the Millennium Dome for the Millennium exhibition. This exhibition was not the hoped-for success, however, so the service was short-lived.

Thames Clippers' 220-seat *Hurricane Clipper* (2002) is seen between Hungerford and Waterloo bridges in July 2003. She was working a 'Tate to Tate' service between the then recently opened Tate Modern and Tate Britain galleries. At the time she carried a special 'dots' livery to promote a David Hockney art exhibition at the Tate Modern. The Thames Clipper catamarans were built in Australia.

In July 2005 *Storm Clipper* (1999) departs from Woolwich Arsenal Pier, the eastwards limit of Thames Clippers services. The pier at Woolwich opened in 2002. The Royal Arsenal itself had closed in 1967 and the Ministry of Defence finally finished with the site in 1994, since when the site has been redeveloped as Royal Arsenal Riverside with housing and amenities.

Greenwich Pier is an important stop on the Thames Clippers route. Here, *Tornado Clipper* (2007) makes a call. In the foreground one of the older, smaller vessels is providing a taxi service to the Silverseas Cruises Ltd cruise ship *Silver Whisper* [Nassau], anchored close by on Greenwich Ship Tier.

Near Wapping, and *Cyclone Clipper* (2007) is pulling into a pier.

Taken from on board the paddle steamer *Waverley*, *Hurricane Clipper* again heads downriver against a backdrop of Tower Bridge and some of the City of London skyscrapers on 6 October 2017.

Cross River Ferries

There are long-established ferry crossings at Woolwich and Tilbury. The Woolwich Free Ferry dates back to 1884, when the Metropolitan Board of Works proposed a free passenger and vehicle ferry between the north and south banks of the River Thames at Woolwich. There was already a passenger ferry service here – indeed there had been a ferry crossing here for hundreds of years. The coming of the railway age saw the first railway in London linking London with Greenwich. But Parliament would not allow the extension of the railway on to the important town of Woolwich with its army garrison and arsenal. This was because the railway would have to tunnel under Maze Hill and they were concerned that this work might upset the workings of Greenwich Observatory, from where Greenwich Mean Time was set, which was adopted by the Railway Clearing House in 1847 to become standard railway time. So the Eastern Counties & Thames Junction Railway saw an opportunity and built a rail line from Stratford to North Woolwich on the opposite bank. They then commenced their own ferry service across the river.

By the time the free ferry started in March 1889, the Metropolitan Board of Works had become replaced by the London County Council, who continued to maintain the service. This soon killed off the railway's ferry. In October 1912, a foot tunnel was built under the river to supplement the ferry or provide pedestrian access when the ferry was not running.

The original ferries were replaced by four new steam paddle ferries. *Squires* and *Gordon* were built at Cowes in 1922–3 and *John Benn* and *Will Crooks* in 1930. These impressive vessels measured 166 feet by 44 feet. They could carry 1,000 passengers and up to 100 tons of vehicles. Their paddles were independently driven to maximise manoeuvrability. The boilers of the two separate engines burnt coke produced at the nearby Beckton gas works.

The steam ferries lasted until 1963, when they were replaced by three diesel vessels built by the Caledon Shipbuilding & Engineering Company, Dundee. These had two Voith Schneider propulsion units each, one at each end. They could carry 200 tons of vehicles but only some 500 passengers. They were named after prominent local politicians *Ernest Bevin*, *John Burns* and *James Newman*. At first these continued to use the old loading linkspan piers and so were side-loading like their predecessors. But in 1966 new piers were opened that allowed for the more convenient end-loading 'drive-on/drive-off' procedure.

The London County Council was replaced by the Greater London Council in 1965. When this was abolished in 1985 the ferry management became the responsibility of the London Borough of Greenwich (now the Royal Borough of Greenwich), latterly on behalf of Transport for London. But their involvement ended in 2008 and, after a period when it was run by Serco, Briggs Marine now operate the ferry on behalf of TfL.

Although with the closure of the Royal docks in 1983, the number of passengers using the ferries and tunnel has declined, the ferry remains important as one of the few vehicle crossing points in East London. Normally two ferries were used on weekdays, with one at weekends. But after fifty-five years they were considered life-expired and so two new vessels were ordered in 2016 to replace them. These have been built by Polish company Remontowa. They are diesel-electric hybrid vessels. As well as carrying cars and lorries, they have dedicated space for cyclists and can carry 150 passengers.

A ferry crossing between Gravesend and Tilbury has existed since medieval times and is mentioned in the Domesday Book. Gravesend Corporation ran a ferry for which they built the Town Pier in 1834. In 1854 the London, Tilbury & Southend Railway reached Tilbury and commenced their own ferry service, later taking over the Corporation service and Town Pier in 1864. The service in due course passed to British Railways' Sealink subsidiary. Sealink was sold off in 1984 and sold on in 1990 to Stena Line. Then, in 1991, White Horse Ferries took over the service and replaced the ageing ex-BR ferry *Edith* with a catamaran they constructed locally themselves in 1992. The service has changed hands twice since then.

A passenger ferry used to carry Ford's staff from their Dagenham plant to the south bank near Belvedere. This was a free service started in 1933, which, at its peak, carried up to 2,000 passengers a week. Latterly the service was operated by R&G Passenger Launches with three catamarans, the *Twinstar I, II* and *III*. When Ford gave up car manufacture at Dagenham, in favour of building engines, the service was withdrawn from 30 January 2004, by which time only 250–300 workers were using it each week.

More recently, the Hilton Ferry has linked Canary Wharf Pier, on the Isle of Dogs, with Hilton Docklands Nelson Dock Pier, at Rotherhithe, on the south bank since September 2004. This is run by Thames Clippers and operates every twenty minutes (ten minutes peak hours). An earlier service on this route had been operated by White Horse Ferries.

In 1963 the four steam paddle ferries on the Woolwich crossing were replaced by three diesel ferries built by the Caledon Shipbuilding & Engineering Co., Dundee. Like their predecessors, they were named after local politicians. *Ernest Bevin* was at the linkspan on the south side of the river in 2004.

Ernest Bevin again, in mid-river during 2014. Note the 'Mayor of London' banner and Transport for London roundel now applied.

In their last month of service, *James Newman* makes another crossing on 26 September 2018.

A sad sight! Against a backdrop of the London Docklands skyline (Canary Wharf towers, O2 Arena, etc.), Woolwich ferry *James Newman* leaves Woolwich for the last time, under tow by French tug *TSM Kermor* (Brest). On the right, *Sider Venture* can be seen unloading at the Tate & Lyle Thames Refinery wharf. It is shortly after 9.00 a.m. on 25 October 2018.

Later the same morning the pair are seen from Erith pier as they make their way down the Thames and eventually across the Channel to Le Havre. Ferry *John Burns* had been the first to go on Sunday 7 October. The tug would be back later for *Ernest Bevin* – the last of the old ferries to leave the Thames – on 31 October.

One of the new ferries, *Ben Woollacott*, undergoes a loaded test run on 28 January 2019. This vessel is named after a nineteen-year-old deckhand who drowned after being dragged overboard while working on the ferries.

A number of buses were supplied by Ensignbus for the loaded test, and here we see the unusual sight of ex-London Routemasters disembarking. While no bus routes cross on the ferry, they are often used for transferring double-decker buses between garages north and south of the river. Otherwise they would have to travel via Tower Bridge as the Blackwall Tunnel can only take single-deck vehicles.

The new ferries finally entered service in February 2019. Both ferries are seen in use on 25 March. The other ferry is named *Dame Vera Lynn*, after the legendary singer, who came from East Ham.

White Horse Ferries Ltd acquired the Gravesend–Tilbury ferry service in 1991 from Stena Line, who in turn had acquired it from Sealink. From 1996 the regular ferry was the *Martin Chuzzlewit*, one of a small number of vessels built by the company themselves from 1992 and named after characters from Charles Dickens novels. This was a water jet trimaran powered by a Perkins diesel engine and could carry fifty passengers.

After the demise of White Horse Ferries, from 10 June 2002 the service was taken over by Captain John Potter, who used the *Duchess M* [Portsmouth], a former Gosport–Portsmouth ferry dating from 1956.

Whenever she was unavailable, Captain Potter would employ his other vessel, the excursion craft *Princess Pocahontas*.

The ferry operated from the ferry pier at Gravesend, where the former vehicle ferries had plied before they were replaced by the Dartford Tunnel. Both the *Duchess M* and *Princess Pocahontas* are on the pier in this view. Tilbury Power Station is across the river.

Duchess M is seen in the later style of livery on 15 March 2017. From 2012 the ferry service moved to the new Town Pier pontoon.

From May 2017 Jet Stream Tours of Strood took over the service. Their *Thames Swift* (1996) was no stranger, being formerly on the service with White Horse Ferries as the *Martin Chuzzlewit*. She was photographed on a test run prior to entering service on 25 April 2017.

When *Thames Swift* is unavailable, their back-up vessel is the *Jacob Marley* [Rochester], built in 1985 as the *Condor Kestrel* for Condor Ferries in the Channel Islands. This vessel is seen in use in June 2019.

A ferry used to link Ford's plant at Dagenham with the south bank at Belvedere. This view from April 2002 shows the south bank pier.

One of the regular ferries in use was the *Twin Star*, seen making the crossing in April 2002. *Twin Star* had a capacity for 120 passengers.

In 2004 the Ford ferry ceased and the *Twin Star* was acquired by Thames Clippers as the ferry for the Hilton Ferry service between the Isle of Dogs and Rotherhithe, where there is a Hilton hotel.

The *Twin Star*, seen arriving at the Rotherhithe pier on 24 September 2018. Note the revised livery.

Hotel

Unlike the cruise ships that visit London, this ship won't take you anywhere. The *Sunborn London* is a static floating hotel which, since 2014, has been moored in the Royal Victoria Dock, close to the ExCel exhibition centre. It replaced an earlier floating hotel, the *Sunborn*, which came in 2002.

Tourist Excursion Craft, Etc.

The tourist market continues to be catered for with regular trips from Central London to Greenwich. There is also a limited service to the west side of London, while local excursions operate around Richmond, Kingston and Hampton Court. Further west, Windsor is another major tourist area where local river trips do good business.

In the early part of the new century there were still some venerable vessels employed on the tourist trade through Central London. City Cruises' *Vita*, seen in October 2001, was a former Portsmouth–Gosport ferry dating from 1960.

City Cruises also ran the *Witheycombe*, seen loading on Festival Pier by the Royal Festival Hall in March 2000.

By contrast the City Cruises 'Millennium class' catamarans, introduced, as the name implies, in 2000, could not look more different. They are the mainstay of the fleet and *Millennium Dawn* is at Greenwich Pier in April 2013. The pier was upgraded in the early 2000 with disabled access and new ticketing and catering facilities.

A more recent arrival, the *Millennium Diamond* (2012), is seen at Tower Pier in September 2017. This can carry 600 passengers or 200 diners.

A general view of the Upper Pool with various moored tourist boats and HMS *Belfast* in February 2013.

At St Katharine Pier, just to the east of Tower Bridge, the *Sarpedon* calls in May 2019. Built for Crown River Cruises in 2001, this 400-seater vessel cost £1 million plus.

Charing Cross Pier in June 2006 with vessels of Bateaux London. The *Pridela* is nearest.

We saw the *Princess Pocahontas* earlier in use on the Tilbury–Gravesend ferry service (see p. 27). Her normal duties were trips to London or Southend and here she is approaching Charing Cross on 10 July 2002. She was built in Germany in 1962 and licensed for 300 passengers. She came to the Thames in 1989.

There are also night tours and party boat trips. This is Tower Pier at night with *The Wyndham* docking. The Tower of London is illuminated in the background and part of Tower Bridge, also lit up, can be seen. This photograph was taken from the *Waverley* on arrival back at London on 6 October 2017.

Amongst the vessels that operate predominantly during the evening are the *Dixie Queen*, a mock Mississippi paddle steamer, and the *Elizabethan* and *Edwardian* of Thames Luxury Charters. The three vessels are on their daytime berth, in the Lower Pool, in April 2019. The *Dixie Queen* is the largest tourist excursion craft on the Thames, capable of carrying some 700 passengers. She started out as a roll-on, roll-off ferry linking Stockholm with local islands, before being converted as Sweden's largest floating nightclub. She came to the Thames in the late 1990s.

The oldest excursion craft on the Thames is probably the *Yarmouth Belle*, owned by Turk Launches. Built in 1892, in Great Yarmouth, she originally operated between Yarmouth and Norwich on the River Yare, before coming to new owners on the Thames in 1946. Turk Launches acquired her in 1988 and have since fitted dummy paddle wheels and funnel. She is now used for cruises and charters. She is seen at St Helena Pier, in Richmond, in July 2009.

The *Yarmouth Belle* sets out on a trip with a reasonable complement of passengers on deck. In July 2019, the BBC London news reported that the fate of some of the oldest River Thames excursion craft might be in jeopardy because proposed new safety regulations would require prohibitively expensive modifications.

Windsor is another place where tourist craft operate all year round. Yet another mock American stern wheel paddle steamer, the *Southern Comfort*, passes through in February 2019 with the castle prominent in the distance. Note the twin funnel structure in its lowered position to provide clearance under bridges. Windsor is beyond the limit of the tidal Thames and the PLA jurisdiction (which is at Teddington).

This is perhaps an appropriate point to mention those craft whose function is to cater for tourists (and Londoners) in a static capacity. The former Humber ferry *Tattershall Castle* [Grimsby] (1934, 556 tonnes) was withdrawn in 1972 and has been moored by Hungerford Bridge as a floating pub/restaurant since 1982. This is how she looked in March 2000.

Unfortunately, a refit at Yarmouth in 2003–4 saw her lose many of her original features including the bridge superstructure and paddle wheels. This was the result in June 2004.

The former River Clyde excursion craft, latterly in the fleet of Caledonian MacBrayne, *Queen Mary* (1933, 1,014 tonnes) also came to the Thames in 1988 as a restaurant ship, bought by Bass Charrington to replace the fire-damaged *Old Caledonia* (see p. 7). During the years when the Cunard liner *Queen Mary* was operational, she carried the name *Queen Mary II*. She is seen at Waterloo Bridge in March 2000.

In 2005 she received this controversial blue/black livery. Thankfully she reverted to black and white the following year.

On 9 November 2009 *Queen Mary* was towed away from her mooring on the Embankment and eventually taken into Tilbury Dock. Here she remained laid up for several years before being sold abroad. Here she was near the beginning of her journey along the river, being towed towards Blackfriars Bridge and passing HMS *President*. The funnels were removed to allow clearance under the bridges.

River Shipping Support Services

Tugs – Ship Handling

A number of different companies have provided tugs for ship towage on the Thames over the years. The famous name of Sun Tugs (W. H. J. Alexander Ltd) had become Alexandra Towing in 1975 and then passed to Howard Smith Towage in March 1993. They in turn passed to Adsteam (UK) Ltd in August 2001. This was an Australian company, the name deriving from the former Adelaide Steamship Co. In 2007 the Adsteam group passed to Svitzer Marine, who continue to provide tugs at Tilbury for the Thames and also at Sheerness for the River Medway. At busy times these will work in each other's 'territory'. Since 2013, Svitzer have had competition from the Dutch-owned operator KOTUG who normally have four or five tugs based on the Thames.

From 29 August 2019, KOTUG Smit Towage was sold to the Spanish-owned Boluda Group and now trades as Boluda Towage UK. New funnel markings are now in place.

Adsteam (UK) Ltd tug *Shorne* [London] was one of a pair built in 1984 for the Dover Harbour Board as *Deft* and *Dextrous*. In 2000 they passed to Howard Smith Towage for use on the Thames and were renamed *Shorne* and *Cobham*. She retained Howard Smith colours when photographed at Gravesend on 14 February 2002.

Adsteam Towage *Sun Anglia* [London] (1985, 336 tonnes) was new to Alexandra Towing, passing to Howard Smith Towage and then to Adsteam, where she later became *Adsteam Anglia*. She would in turn pass to Svitzer and become *Svitzer Anglia*. This photograph was taken on 26 June 2003.

In 2003 Adsteam Marine transferred two tugs from their Australian operations to the UK River Thames setup. These were the *Redcliffe* (1986) and *Gurrong* (2000). The *Redcliffe* [London] is seen here on 9 September 2003. She was later renamed *Adsteam Redcliffe* while the *Gurrong* became *Adsteam Victory* in 2005 and was transferred to the River Medway at Sheerness.

Adsteam Towage's *Lady Cecilia* [Grimsby] was transferred to the Thames after previously working at Immingham. She is seen on 2 August 2005.

A pair of former Alexandra Towing tugs, now renamed the *Adsteam Mercia* (1990) and *Adsteam Sussex* (1992), return to base after another job on 30 July 2006. As *Sun Sussex*, this had been the last new tug delivered to Alexandra Towing before their takeover.

In 2007 Adsteam were taken over by Svitzer Marine so it would be a new name and livery for what now became *Svitzer Mercia*, seen here in 2014.

Tugs were also based at Sheerness on the River Medway and whenever it got particularly busy, tugs from the Medway would help out at Tilbury or vice versa. *Svitzer Brenda* (formerly Adsteam Towage's *Lady Brenda*) is one of the tugs normally based on the Medway but is seen in use at Tilbury on 14 August 2011.

From time to time, Svitzer replace the Thames-based tugs with new ones or tugs transferred in from elsewhere in the country. *Svitzer Adira* had previously been working at Southampton when it arrived in 2018 and is registered there.

A group of four Svitzer tugs lay over off Denton, Gravesend, while awaiting their next call to duty in 2014.

In 2003 BP Shipping decided to purchase three tugs to serve the Coryton oil terminal. Built in Holland and registered on the Isle of Man, these came in 2005 and were named *Castle Point*, *Corringham* and *Stanford*. *Corringham* [Douglas] is seen on 29 September 2005. The Coryton terminal closed in 2012, after which the *Castle Point* and *Stanford* were sold to Svitzer and transferred elsewhere, while the *Corringham* was retained by BP Shipping but transferred to Scotland.

From 2013 Svitzer have had competition from Kotug, who have based around four or five tugs on the Thames. This is *ZP Bear* [Valletta] on 25 September 2015.

Another view of *ZP Bear*, emerging from the Royal Docks on 16 October 2016.

Kotug's *SD Seal* (2008) approaches Tower Bridge, after assisting the visiting *St Helena* up the Thames, to moor alongside HMS *Belfast* on a courtesy visit (see p. 69) on 7 June 2016.

The Kotug tugs usually assemble on Tilbury Landing Stage when it is not in use by a cruise ship and here a representative selection are in place in September 2018, including *SD Seal* and *RT Dolphin*.

Bugsier Tugs are a major German operator, particularly in Hamburg and Bremerhaven. In March 2019 Bugsier tug *Bugsier 10* [Hamburg] was working for Svitzer at Tilbury. Here she is seen on 11 March.

Bunkering

A small fleet was maintained by TSS (Thames Shipping Services Ltd). The *Tommy* (1963, 315 tonnes) and *Torduct* (1959, 100 tonnes) are lashed together here as they proceed upriver on 2 March 2007. A bulk carrier is on Tilbury Power Station.

The largest vessel in the TSS fleet was the *K. Toulson* (1966, 833 tonnes), photographed on 28 June 2006. Like the *Tommy*, she had come from the fleet of Bowker & King Ltd, where she had been the *Beechcroft*.

With the demise of TSS, other vessels have been used to fill the void. *Culex* [Freetown] was with Allantone Supplies Ltd when seen on 9 May 2013.

A stern view of *Culex*. She was built in 1968 by Babcock Marine of Appledore.

The *Conveyer* [Hull] (1980, 307 tonnes) is another vessel of Allantone Supplies Ltd that has been used on bunkering, seen in 2016. This had previously been used by TSS under the same name.

Currently active on the Thames is the *Distributor*, seen at Gravesend in 2019.

A small vessel that can pass under the Thames bridges and bunker the tourist craft is the *Karolien*, seen at Gravesend in 2015. She is owned by Karolien River Fuels Ltd.

Port of London Authority

A familiar sight for many years was the PLA pilot launch *Patrol*, carrying river pilots to and from ships at Tilbury, in September 2013.

In 2019 this has been replaced by a new launch, the *Guide*, seen on 29 March.

The PLA has a number of other launches for aspects of its work. This is survey launch *Verifier* [London] in 2015.

The *Royal Nore* [London], a rather more upmarket launch in the PLA fleet, perhaps used for transporting corporate guests and dignitaries. She was at the Tower of London when seen in 2014.

The PLA vessels are based at Royal Terrace Pier, Gravesend. This view of the pier in 2018 shows some of their launches moored up.

The PLA used to own a trio of general-purpose/salvage vessels that could be used to do such jobs as maintaining buoys or removing debris from the river. This is *Hookness*, in the old green livery, passing Gravesend on 14 February 2002.

Crossness, in faded blue livery, moored at Woolwich on 21 January 2006.

These have been replaced by the *London Titan*, launched in 2015, a name formerly carried by one of the PLA's floating cranes. She is seen passing Gravesend on 30 March 2017. She was built by Manor Marine of Portland, Dorset, carries a crew of five, and is low enough and with sufficient draught to operate as far upriver as Richmond.

A pair of PLA driftwood collection vessels, *Driftwood I* and *II*, moored up at Woolwich near the Thames flood barrier in 2014.

Pusher driftwood tug *Impulse* pushes a PLA lighter past Gravesend on 25 February 2008.

An unusual task for *Impulse*. On 24 March 2004 she towed a very large 2,210 dwt docking barge for heavy transport specialists Robert Wynn & Sons upriver and was photographed having just passed under Waterloo bridge. The barge was to collect the fuselage of a Concorde aircraft, G-BOAA, from Isleworth, 90 miles from the PLA's seaward limit. This was then to be transported around the coast to Torness near Dunbar. From there it was to be taken by road to the Museum of Flight, East Fortune, near Edinburgh.

Other Specialist Services

Port Health Authority motor launch *Lady Aileen* approaches Gravesend pier on 13 August 2003. This vessel was still in use in 2018. This is a service provided by the Corporation of the City of London.

The PLA manage the Thames Oil Spill Clearance Association (TOSCA), established in 1992 to collect and contain oil in the event of a river spillage. The recovery launch *Recover* is a purpose-built catamaran fitted with equipment to collect and store polluting oil. She was seen at Gravesend in 2014.

TSS, whose bunkering tankers we saw earlier, also had a pair of tankers to supply fresh water to vessels in dock. The *Aquatic* [London] (1963, 315 tonnes) was seen on 23 September 2003. The other vessel was the *Aquaduct* (1964, 908 tonnes).

Tidy Thames Co. have two vessels, *Tidy Thames I* and *II*, to collect floating debris from the river. *Tidy Thames I* approaches Tower Bridge past the entrance to St Katharine's Dock in July 2011.

London Fire Brigade fire rescue craft *Firedart* near Waterloo Bridge in 2001.

To maintain water quality in the Thames, Thames Water have this 'bubbler' craft, *Thames Vitality* (1997), which can pump up to 30 tonnes of oxygen into the river where needed. It was noted near Westminster Bridge in June 2000.

GPS Services are one of the main operators of lighterage tugs on the rivers Thames and Medway. They also have this heavy-lift floating crane, *GPS Apollo*, which was photographed passing Gravesend on 14 August 2011 carrying a suction elevator from one of the dockside wharves.

Another heavy lift floating crane, the *Taklift 3*, has been towed upriver to Central London (obviously with the jib folded down flat to pass under the bridges). Now it is engaged in some task near Hungerford Bridge and is moored on Festival Pier on 22 May 2002.

A multi-purpose work boat fitted with a telescopic crane, the *Multrasalvor 3* was approaching Gravesend pier on 11 August 2013.

Shakedog is a similar type of vessel and was seen in the same location but travelling the opposite way on 25 May 2017. The redundant Tilbury Power Station in the background has since been demolished.

Courtesy Visits, Etc.

Naval Vessels

'Relax, it's one of ours' – Royal Navy L14 HMS *Albion* arrives at Gravesend on 12 July 2006. Referred to as an amphibious transport dock, *Albion* and sister ship *Bulwark* were launched in 2001.

German navy corvette F264 *Ludwigshafen am Rhein* passing Gravesend on a courtesy visit in 2015.

Royal Navy aircraft carrier HMS *Ark Royal* was a visitor to Greenwich for six days in 2004 for a courtesy visit, including promoting the Sea Cadets. She was escorted safely through the Thames Barrier with the help of four tugs and is seen here at Greenwich on 29 February 2004.

Royal Navy assault ship L12 HMS *Ocean* was sited at Greenwich during the Olympic Games as part of the security against possible acts of terrorism. She is seen on 5 August 2012.

A802 HNLMS *Snellius* was moored by the Excel Centre in Royal Victoria Dock on 22 March 2004. She is a hydrographic survey vessel for the Royal Netherlands Navy.

Royal Navy frigate F229 HMS *Lancaster* is a tight fit as she is brought through the lock, into West India Dock, by tug *Svitzer Mercia* for a courtesy visit on 2 March 2013.

The UK Border Agency is charged with the responsibility for securing our shores against illegal immigrants. A number of patrol craft are operated and here *Seeker* is on the Thames at Gravesend.

An unusual vessel making a courtesy visit in July 2002, the *Kojima* belonged to the Japan Coast Guard. She was berthed in West India Dock during her stay.

Other Vessels

Educational Book Exhibits Ltd ran this charity book exhibition ship, *Logos II* [Valletta] (1968, 4804 tonnes), which was a visitor open to the public in West India Dock in early September 2001. She had previously been a Spanish-owned ferry, the *Antonio Lazaro*, until acquired in 1988. She was sold for breaking in Turkey in 2009.

For a later visit on 19 June 2009, Operation Mobilisation Logos, the Christian outreach parent company of Educational Book Exhibits Ltd, had acquired the *Logos Hope* [Torshavn] (1973, 7927 tonnes). This was a former German-owned ferry, the *Noronna*, which had been withdrawn in 2004 and was refitted for her new role in 2005.

Peace Boat are a Japan-based international NGO working to promote peace, human rights and sustainability. They organise global voyages to promote their aims. The *Olvia* [Odessa] is seen approaching the entrance to West India Dock on 18 June 2002. This was one of five ships of the Belorussiya class, built in 1975–6 for the Black Sea Shipping Company as cruiseferries but later adapted for cruising. Originally the *Kareliya*, she passed to K&O Shipping for use by Peace Boat in 2001.

Norwegian-owned Hertigruten ship *Fram* [Narvik] returns past Gravesend after a courtesy visit to London on 25 April 2009. She had also visited London when new in 2007. Hertigruten operate along the Norwegian coast and to the various coastal islands.

The *St Helena*, owned by St Helena Line Ltd, was the ship providing the link between Cape Town and the remote British island of St Helena, with some journeys continuing to Ascension Island. A new airport on St Helena was due to make this redundant and she made a courtesy visit to London in 2016 before being decommissioned. Here she is seen arriving at Tower Bridge assisted by Kotug tug *ZP Bear* on 7 June 2016. This ship was one of the last two to carry the title Royal Mail Ship, and was built by Hall, Russell & Co., Aberdeen, in 1989 (6,767 tonnes), with capacity for 128 passengers and 1,800 tonnes of cargo.

Unfortunately, the airport was declared unsafe due to strong crosswinds and the ship had to continue in use. It was eventually opened in October 2017 and the *St Helena* decommissioned. The ship then made a return visit to London, arriving on 30 January 2019, and is seen approaching Woolwich in the early morning light. The coat of arms had been removed from the funnel sides. The vessel was subsequently sold to new owners.

The *Stubnitz* [Rostock] was a former East German fish factory ship that, since 1993, has been converted as a venue for live music, exhibitions, performances and media art by Motorschiff Stubnitz, a non-profit organisation. She has travelled to many European countries since then and spent a period in London at West India Dock in 2013, where she was photographed on 17 February.

The *Discovery*, an exploration/research ship operated in conjunction with the University of Southampton, approaches Gravesend, returning from a courtesy visit to London.

Seen in the Royal Docks lock on 19 April 2005, the cable ship *C.S. Sovereign*, owned by Global Marine Systems Ltd, visited the Excel Centre, London, as part of Ship Week 2005. Ships can only pass from the lock to the Royal Albert and Royal Victoria Docks (for the Excel Centre) at night because of the need to leave height clearance during flying times for the runway at London City Airport, which lies between the King George V Dock and these docks.

Offshore installation support vessels *Siem Moxie* and *Atlantic Enterprise* at the Excel Centre, visiting in connection with an exhibition being held there in 2017.

The *Resolution* [Douglas] (2003, 7,000 tonnes) was designed for installing offshore wind turbines. On a courtesy visit to London for the British Wind Energy Association in February 2005, she moored in the Lower Pool – she was presumably too high to pass through Tower Bridge. When on site at a wind farm, the six legs are lowered to the sea bed, allowing the ship to withstand a Force 12 hurricane and 14-metre waves. She can carry up to ten wind turbines and has accommodation for thirty-six installation personnel in addition to her crew.

Laid Up

The former Radio Caroline pirate radio ship *Ross Revenge* was laid up at Tilbury Docks for nine years. Here she is seen at the landing stage on 7 October 2004. She left Tilbury in July 2014 and is now moored on the River Blackwater, near Bradwell, where she is once again transmitting (legally!).

A stern view of the Radio Caroline ship taken on 7 October 2004. She had originally been built as a fishing trawler, but with the decline in fishing she was sold off and eventually acquired for Radio Caroline in 1983, where she served until being shipwrecked on the Goodwin Sands.

This sea-going catamaran, the *Sea Leopard*, had spent a period laid up in Tilbury Dock prior to her departure on 9 August 2009.

Oil drilling ship *Sertao* (2012) spent 2018 laid up and for sale at Tilbury Power Station. She was built for a Brazilian company that went bankrupt in 2015, leading to her being repossessed. She was eventually towed away for further storage at Port Talbot on 25 February 2019. This was to allow the final demolition of the power station and for work to then start on the Tilbury 2 project to redevelop the area as an expansion of the port.

Sailing ships

Sail Training ships

The Sail Training Association (now the Tall Ships Youth Trust) brig *Stavros S. Niarchos* near Rainham on 27 September 2000, the year she was built. She was sold in 2017.

These ships often berth in West India Dock and the visit of the Argentine Navy sail training ship *Libertad* on 4 August 2002 proved no exception. This fully rigged ship was ordered in 1956 and built in Rio Santiago, Buenos Aires.

The Rendez-Vous 2017 Tall Ships Regatta started from Greenwich in April 2017 and brought a wide variety of sailing ships to the river. The Sea Cadets TS *Royalist* was amongst these and was seen here moored at Woolwich along with other visiting craft on 13 April 2017.

Among the other ships arriving for the Tall Ships Regatta was the Norwegian sail training ship *Christian Radich*, anchored on Greenwich Ship Tier on 16 April.

Dutch sailing barque *Artemis* (1926) also came over for the 2017 Tall Ships Regatta and is seen at Woolwich. Interestingly, she started out as a Norwegian whale-catcher, being converted to her present form in around 2001 for hospitality and corporate functions. She has been a frequent visitor to the Thames since then.

Other Sailing Ships

In 2012, Olympics year, and again in 2014, several Dutch-owned sailing ships came to the Thames for a week or two, offering trips between Greenwich and Woolwich piers. One of these, the *J. R. Tolkien*, lays over at Woolwich on 11 September 2014.

Another of the vessels participating, the *Oosterschelde*, approaches Woolwich on a trip on the same day.

One of the smaller vessels, the *Zephyr*, approaching Woolwich on 15 April 2017.

Two ships, including the *Pedro Doncker* [Amsterdam], lay over at Greenwich in April 2017.

Historic Replicas

In November 2006, the Museum of London Docklands at West India Dock played host to a replica of the *Discovery*, the smallest of three ships that sailed from Blackwall on the Thames to establish the first permanent English settlement at Jamestown, Virginia, in 1606.

The notice board explaining the history of the *Discovery* and its replica.

Somewhat larger was the *Gotheburg*, built in Sweden in 2005 as a replica of an eighteenth-century East Indiaman merchant ship. The original ship sank outside the port of Gothenburg in September 1745, in what has since been thought to be an insurance scam. The replica set out on a voyage from Sweden to China and back, calling at London from 19 May to 2 June 2007 as the last stop on the return journey. Here she was entering West India Dock on 19 May 2007.

Another replica, the Portuguese caravel *Vera Cruz*, passing Gravesend on 10 April 2017. As can be seen, this is running under motor power, a fixture that would not have been available on the original vessels of this type! She was built in 2002 for sail training.

Thames Barges

Thames barge *Hydrogen*, seen under sail and with passengers enjoying a cruise on board. She was photographed near Woolwich on 30 June 2002.

Stern detail of *Hydrogen*, photographed while moored at the Greenwich Pier pontoon in 2014. She is a wooden-hulled barge built at Rochester in 1906.

A series of barge races take place through the summer months at various locations around the Essex coast and rivers. Gravesend is one of the starting locations. On 28 June 2003 barges are lining up for the start, with the *Phoenician* (1922) in the foreground.

Crew members working on *Adieu* (built 1929), on 21 June 2019, while moored at the Gravesend Pier pontoon for the 2019 barge race. One of the Grimaldi Line container/vehicle carriers can be seen on the Tilbury Ro-Ro berth.

Several Thames barges can usually be found moored inside St Katharine Docks. Here, on 15 November 2004, *Lady Daphne*, built at Rochester in 1923, is in the foreground.

On 9 May 2011, Thames barge *Dawn* arrived at St Katharine Docks with a deck cargo of hay. She had been loaded, possibly on the River Blackwater, and sailed down the Essex coast for a TV programme about old trade routes. On arrival, part of the cargo was taken by horse and cart to one of the London cavalry barracks, again as part of the programme. On a chance visit to the dock the next day, I discovered the remainder of *Dawn*'s cargo being unloaded.

Deckhands shift the bales of hay from the deck of *Dawn*. These were removed by motor vehicle – the TV film crews had finished their work. *Dawn* was built in 1897 as a 'stackie' for the hay market. She has been restored as the only working full-sized tiller-steered Thames barge.

Many of the Thames barges were motorised in later life, and almost all of those in preservation are so fitted. One of only three that still rely on sail power alone is the bowsprit barge *Edme* (1898), which is seen tacking her way up the river in September 2017.

Other Heritage Shipping

Most famous of the heritage ships to be found in Central London is the cruiser HMS *Belfast*, in the Pool of London between Tower Bridge and London Bridge. Built by Harland & Wolff and commissioned in 1939, she took part in Arctic convoys, the Battle of North Cape (which resulted in the sinking of the German battlecruiser *Scharnhorst*), and provided gunfire support for the Normandy D-Day landings. She has been based at her present location since 1971, under the ownership of the Imperial War Museum since 1978, and is open to the public.

Moored between Temple Pier and Blackfriars Bridge, on Victoria Embankment, are two former Royal Navy escort vessels. HMS *President* was built by Lobnitz at Renfrew in 1918 as the Anchusa class sloop HMS *Saxifrage*, armed with two 4-inch guns for escorting convoys. Laid up in 1920, she was refitted for a new career as a training ship for London Division RNVR, renamed and took up her post in 1922. When a new land-based headquarters was built in 1988, she became redundant and was sold as a function/conference venue.

In 2014 HMS *President* was given this 'Dazzle ship' camouflage livery, as used during the First World War, the centenary of which was being celebrated. This vessel was subsequently moved to Chatham Docks in 2016 because of the construction of the new Thames Tideway Tunnel.

HMS *Wellington*, seen here in 2018, was built in 1934 at Devonport. Her wartime service included convoy escort duties in the North Atlantic. She was purchased in 1947 by the Honourable Company of Master Mariners and converted into a floating Livery Hall. In 2005, ownership was transferred to the Wellington Trust to ensure the continued preservation of the vessel.

There can be few less famous ships than the *Cutty Sark*. Built as a tea clipper in 1869, she survived by virtue of later being used as a static training ship. She arrived at Greenwich for preservation in a dry dock in 1954. Disaster struck during renovation when a fire broke out on 21 May 2007, apparently caused by an industrial vacuum cleaner left running throughout the weekend. Although there was extensive damage, much of the timber had been removed from the ship for restoration and so was not affected. The renovation has seen the ship now raised on steel props and the hull controversially enclosed. This view shows the ship before the restoration work started.

The steam tug *Portwey* [Falmouth] was built by Harland & Wolff Ltd at Govan on the River Clyde and delivered in 1928 to the Portland & Weymouth Coaling Co. Ltd. She later moved to Dartmouth and then to the Falmouth Docks & Engineering Co. Ltd in 1951. She was withdrawn and sold for preservation in 1967. In 1982 she was donated to the Maritime Trust, London, and from 2000 has been in the care of the Steam Tug Portwey Trust and is normally kept in West India Dock. *Portwey* is coal-fired and has a pair of compound steam engines of 330 ihp. She was seen in steam off Woolwich in 2014.

The London International Boat Show was held at the Excel Centre on the north bank of the former Royal Victoria Dock from 2004 until 2018. In 2005 preserved tugs *Portwey* and *Challenge* were on display there, along with former Victualling Inshore Ship *VIC 56*. The three ships were photographed on 8 January 2005. The *Challenge* was built in 1931 and, when withdrawn in 1973, was the last operational steam tug on the Thames. Sold for preservation, she was moored in St Katharine Docks for nineteen years before being restored to working order in 1995.

Preserved tug *Barking* at Woolwich in 2014. This was built at Faversham in 1928 for the Gas Light & Coke Co., working on the Thames until around 1970. She was rescued from dereliction in 1979 and subsequently restored by 2004. She is now part of the VIC 96 Trust, based at Chatham.

Preserved tug *Kent* at Gravesend Pier pontoon. She was built at Lowestoft in 1948 for J. P. Knight Ltd, London, initially for ship-handling on the River Medway. Withdrawn and put aside in 1987, she was acquired for preservation in 1995 by the South Eastern Tug Society and restored to working order in 1999.

Bow winch details of tug *Kent*. She is normally kept at Chatham.

Coaster *Robin* was built on Bow Creek and launched in May 1890 for a London owner. However, in 1900 she was sold to a company in Bilbao, Spain, as the *Maria*, where she would remain in use until 1974. In 1966 she was converted from coal to oil-firing. On final withdrawal she was purchased by the Maritime Trust, restored, and displayed under her original name at St Katharine Docks. In 1991 she moved to West India Quay, where in 2002, under new ownership, she was equipped as an education centre and gallery. She is seen here on 29 May 2006.

In June 2008 a £1.9 million refit began at Lowestoft. *Robin* is now mounted on a pontoon and displayed in Royal Victoria Dock as a community children's learning centre.

Also in Royal Victoria Dock is the former lightship *LV93*. Built by Philip & Sons, Dartmouth, in 1938, she served at various locations before being sold into private ownership in 2004.

Lightship *LV21* was the last to be constructed by Philip & Sons, being launched in 1963. She served most of her working life off the Kent coast before being decommissioned in 2008. Now privately owned, she has been transformed into a floating art space and performance facility, anchored close to Gravesend Pier. Here she is seen at Gravesend Town Pier pontoon in 2017 while being repainted.

The tug *Knocker White* was built in Holland in 1924 as the *Cairnrock* for Harrisons Lighterage Co., London. She later passed to W. E. White & Sons, Rotherhithe, and was renamed. Converted to diesel in 1960, she was sold for scrap in 1982 but became part of the Museum of London collection in 1984. After the Museum of London Docklands opened in 2003, *Knocker White* was moored outside in West India Dock, although she has since been moved. The stern of the replica *Discovery* can be seen ahead of her bows (see p. 78) in this photograph from 25 November 2006.

Also present was 'tosher' tug *Varlet*. This was built in 1937 by James Pollock & Sons, Faversham, for Vokins & Co. Ltd. She worked in the West India and Royal Docks towing lighters until the early 1980s and is seen on 15 May 2005.

The Thames Diamond Jubilee Pageant was held on 3 June 2012 as part of the Queen's Diamond Jubilee celebrations. A world record of some 670 craft, both current and heritage from tall ships to Dunkirk 'little ships', assembled on the Thames in the Upper and Lower Pools as the Queen and entourage travelled down river on the royal barge *Gloriana*. Here some of the craft are arriving at Tower Bridge on 2 June. Many of the smaller craft had assembled in the West India Dock.

The Victualling Inshore Craft (VIC) was a wartime design based on the Clyde 'puffer', a small cargo ship used in the Western Isles of Scotland. Sixty-three of this 66-foot type were built to service ships at naval bases. Another thirty-five of a longer 80-foot version were also built. Most were coal or oil-fired steamers. Preserved longer types *VIC 56* and *VIC 96* are seen, along with Thames barges, up by London Bridge as part of the pageant.

Royal rowing barge *Gloriana* in St Katharine Docks in 2014. She was privately commissioned and built for the Thames Diamond Jubilee Pageant. She is 90 feet long and powered by eighteen oarsmen. The design was inspired by barges in Canaletto's eighteenth-century London paintings.

Each year since 1978 former River Clyde paddle steamer *Waverley*, owned by the Paddle Steamer Preservation Society, has visited the Thames as part of its programme of trips around the country. She usually stays for around 2–3 weeks in September and October and runs trips to or from Southend, continuing on to or from the Thames forts, the Medway, Clacton, Whitstable, etc. Departure from London is from Tower Pier and on 25 September 2010 she departs from there to head through Tower Bridge on another sailing. HMS *Belfast* is in the background. The tug has turned the *Waverley* and will detach once through the bridge, if not before.

8 October 2011, and Tower Bridge is raised for the *Waverley* as she sails through. *Waverley* was built by A. & J. Inglis Ltd for the London & North Eastern Railway in 1946. In 1951 she was transferred to the Caledonian Steam Packet Co. When withdrawal came in 1973, she was the last sea-going paddle steamer in the world and was sold for a nominal £1 to the Paddle Steamer Preservation Society.

Waverley approaches the Town Pier pontoon at Gravesend en route for London. Since the opening of the pontoon in 2012, *Waverley* calls here rather than at the Tilbury Landing Stage.

Waverley departs from Southend Pier on a return trip to London on 2 October 2008.

The *Balmoral* was built by John I. Thornycroft at Woolston, Southampton, for the Southampton, Isle of Wight & South of England Royal Mail Steam Packet Ltd, better known as Red Funnel. In 1969 she was chartered and later bought by P. & A. Campbell for their Bristol Channel services. Sold in 1980, she later became a floating pub in Dundee before being bought by the Paddle Steamer Preservation Society in 1985. Re-engined and refurbished, she then partnered the *Waverley* in providing tours all around Britain, including on the Thames until 2012. When the Royal Arsenal Pier at Woolwich opened in 2002, she was able to call there and here she is seen at the pier on 7 July 2003.

For many years preserved former River Dart paddle steamer *Kingswear Castle*, built in 1924 by Philip & Sons, Dartmouth, was based at Rochester and ran trips on the Medway from Chatham Historic Dockyard from 1985 onwards. On at least two occasions she ventured onto the Thames and right the way down to London. She did this between 5 and 7 July 2003 to mark twenty years since restoration. On 7 July she was seen pulling away from Woolwich Pier with the Woolwich ferry visible in the background. Unlike the *Waverley*, which is oil-fired, *Kingswear Castle* remains coal-fired.

The *Kingswear Castle* was able to navigate under the Central London bridges, reaching as far west as Putney. Here she approaches Tower Bridge on the return journey on 14 August 2005. The *Kingswear Castle* returned to her former home on the River Dart in 2013.